Valparaiso Public Library
103 Jefferson Street
Valparaiso, IN 46383

PREPARING FOR TOMORROW'S CAREERS™

# POWERING UP A CAREER IN INTERNET SECURITY

**DON RAUF**

ROSEN PUBLISHING
New York

Published in 2016 by The Rosen Publishing Group, Inc.
29 East 21st Street, New York, NY 10010

Copyright © 2016 by The Rosen Publishing Group, Inc.

First Edition

All rights reserved. No part of this book may be reproduced in any form without permission in writing from the publisher, except by a reviewer.

**Library of Congress Cataloging-in-Publication Data**

Rauf, Don, author.
Powering up a career in internet security/Don Rauf.—First edition.
    pages cm.—(Preparing for tomorrow's careers)
Audience: Grades 7 to 12
Includes bibliographical references and index.
ISBN 978-1-4994-6093-3 (library bound)
1. Internet—Vocational guidance—Juvenile literature. 2. Internet—Security measures—Juvenile literature. I. Title.
TK5105.875.I57R386 2016
005.8023-dc23

2015002726

Manufactured in the United States of America

# CONTENTS

Introduction  4

**CHAPTER ONE**
**SAFETY FIRST IN THE INTERNET AGE**  8

**CHAPTER TWO**
**SHARPENING THE MIND FOR A SECURITY CAREER**  23

**CHAPTER THREE**
**STARTING OFF IN A SECURITY CAREER**  33

**CHAPTER FOUR**
**TAKING A STEP UP**  42

**CHAPTER FIVE**
**MEET THE A-TEAM: SECURITY SPECIALISTS**  48

**CHAPTER SIX**
**SECURING A JOB IN INTERNET SECURITY**  56

**CHAPTER SEVEN**
**THE FUTURE OF INTERNET SECURITY**  64

Glossary  69
For More Information  72
For Further Reading  74
Bibliography  76
Index  78

# INTRODUCTION

The Internet links together billions of devices around the globe. While this amazing system has opened up a wealth of information and services to individuals and businesses, it has also made individuals and businesses more exposed and vulnerable. One of the reasons that the Internet has become so popular is because of its ease of access. This same easy connectivity has also made security an ongoing problem.

Many users don't understand how fully available information they transmit or post on the Internet may be. Internet security provides the safeguards to keep information from prying eyes. And Internet security specialists create, maintain, and monitor the systems that keep us safe in the cyber universe. This career area may be referred to as part of IT (information technology) security or sometimes abbreviated to "InfoSec."

Individuals and businesses alike want to make sure that any sensitive

# INTRODUCTION

No one is safe from Internet crime. In 2014, cybercriminals stole private e-mails from Sony Pictures and threatened the company. Even President Obama shared his concerns about the incident.

information (such as financial data) does not fall into the wrong hands. The web, however, can be an access point to materials that are stored on a computer or conveyed via the Internet. When an individual gives credit card information online to make a purchase, he or she wants assurance that Internet security measures are in place to keep that information private. The lucrative world of e-commerce relies on Internet security. If security becomes undependable, this means of doing business would collapse.

Most Internet users are familiar with some protections, such as passwords. From e-mails to bank accounts, passwords give the user a means to protect his or her online information. There are also firewalls, encryption, and many other means of making sure information is seen only by authorized parties.

Computer experts with advanced technological know-how, however, can often break through security measures. In 2014, hackers accessed private e-mails of movie executives at Sony Pictures in response to its movie *The Interview*. These cybercriminals issued threats to Sony if the company were to release the comedy about the assassination of North Korean leader Kim Jong-un.

Although e-mail typically features security blocks to keep such messages from unauthorized viewers, these tech criminals figured out a way to tap into private e-mails and data.

Internet security specialists try to provide protection against web crimes such as these. Computer programmers, software designers, systems analysts, computer crime investigators, educators, monitors, and testers are among those who defend us online. All jobs in this field are in high demand, and the Center for Internet Security and other sources report that the unemployment rate for these trained security professionals has been almost zero.

Major corporations, such as Apple, Microsoft, and Google, are always on the lookout for talented cybersecurity experts. Financial institutions, media groups, and other private businesses all need protection, as do everyday consumers who want to safeguard their identities and financial information. The U.S. government and the military also hire many Internet safety professionals.

The Bureau of Labor Statistics expects continued high employment growth for Internet security specialists and lucrative salaries for those who are most qualified.

In his article "Why Cryptography Is Harder Than It Looks," computer security expert Bruce Schneier said, "History has taught us: never underestimate the amount of money, time, and effort someone will expend to thwart a security system."

So as long as people are out there in the world trying to steal information or cause harm via the Internet, there will be a demand for computer security experts.

## CHAPTER ONE

# SAFETY FIRST IN THE INTERNET AGE

Internet security is a relatively new field because the World Wide Web itself is still a relatively new phenomenon. For many, it's hard to remember that there was a world pre-Internet. Originally, Internet users were interested in accessing and sharing information and e-mailing, but they may not have been thinking of security risks.

We may take the Internet for granted now, but the World Wide Web only became available for public use beginning in 1991. Some use the terms "Internet" and "World Wide Web" interchangeably, but officially the Internet is the network of physical computers that are linked together, while the World Wide Web consists of all the websites that are linked together. Users access the web through their computers via telephone lines, cable lines, and radio waves. Computers in the network called servers store the information and web pages. Software allows us to view websites and web pages and interact with the information and programs.

## THE BASIC BUILDING BLOCKS OF INTERNET ACCESS

On a computer screen, the window to the web is the browser. Some of the top browsers are Mozilla Firefox, Google Chrome, Opera, Safari,

## THE FATHER OF THE WORLD WIDE WEB: TIM BERNERS-LEE

Anyone entering a career in Internet security has one man to thank: the creator of the World Wide Web, Tim Berners-Lee. The idea of the Internet had its inception in 1969 when the U.S. Department of Defense created a system, called the ARPAnet (the Advanced Research Projects Agency network), for its computers to communicate with each other. In 1990, software engineer Berners-Lee came up with the three fundamental technologies that have built the web—HTML, URI, and HTTP. At the time, he was working at CERN, a large particle physics laboratory in Geneva, Switzerland, and communicating with scientists around the world. Berners-Lee sought a fast way for the researchers to share information and saw potential in millions of computers connected together through the Internet. He constructed the first web page and the first web server. In 1993, CERN announced that anyone in the world was allowed to use this World Wide Web technology royalty-free. The World Wide Web Foundation says that Berners-Lee has remained committed to keeping the web free and accessible to everyone. According to the foundation's website, he firmly believes the

*(continued on the next page)*

## THE FATHER OF THE WORLD WIDE WEB: TIM BERNERS-LEE (CONTINUED)

web should be a place where "people can share knowledge, access services, conduct commerce, participate in good governance and communicate in creative way."

and Internet Explorer. The web pages themselves are created with hypertext markup language (HTML), and every web page is actually an HTML file. HTML lets a person design a web page so it can present text, images, links to other web pages, videos, interactive forms, and more.

Over time, web experts have developed other tools that have helped designers build web pages more easily. For example, cascading style sheets (CSS) help "style" web pages, defining how they should look in terms of fonts and colors. To access a specific website, the user puts in a web address or URL (uniform resource locator). A URL is a type of URI (uniform resource identifier). HTTP or hypertext transfer protocol is basically the set of rules for transferring images, text, and information via the web. Web servers understand the HTTP protocol. The server responds when a person opens a browser and connects with a website, using HTTP. A website URL may begin with "http://."

**SAFETY FIRST IN THE INTERNET AGE** | 11

## SIGNS OF SECURITY

Most regular Internet users have seen URLs that begin with "https" as well. The "s" means "secure." This is one of the most fundamental forms of Internet security. When a user is on a page that begins simply with "http://," that site is not secure. Personal information provided on such a site might be viewed by others.

"Https" and the little lock icon mean a website connection is secure and no one else should be able to see information shared on the page.

On the other hand, "https://" indicates a protocol designed to block predators and prying eyes. Websites that ask for credit card information should begin with "https." This means that information transferred between a client (browser) and a website (server) is encrypted.

In contrast, http pages do not have encryption that can stop cybercriminals from stealing personal data. On http sites, the web user has to be careful that he or she has not accessed an imposter site. Some technically savvy criminals set up web pages that mimic those of banks and stores just so they can capture and use the personal financial information.

On a secure bank site, for example, an individual should be directed to a secure https. This page may display a security certificate. This certificate verifies that the website is legitimate and can encrypt information. If the site uses encryption and is officially secure, an icon of a locked padlock may appear in the browser window.

## BEWARE IMPOSTERS

Even security certificates can be forged and used on sites that are impersonating banks, e-retailers, social networks, and other organizations. These phony websites look like they represent legitimate companies. This form of trickery using a fake website is often part of an e-mail scam called phishing. The e-mail entices the recipient to go to a website that may appear legitimate and ask the user to enter personal information. If a criminal gets access to bank accounts through phishing, the finances of an individual or company could be wiped out.

# SAFETY FIRST IN THE INTERNET AGE

Currently, an extended validation certificate (EV) means that a certificate authority has verified that the website is run by a specific organization.

Sometimes the browser will sense that the connection is not secure and display a warning, such as "This Connection Is Untrusted: You have asked Firefox to connect to fakebank.org, but we can't confirm that your connection is secure."

Users constantly have to be vigilant to make sure they are communicating with authentic websites.

For a period of time, the popular online gaming platform Steam did not have certificate checks. Online thieves were able to intercept consumer Paypal payments for months before the company realized and fixed this security hole.

## PASSWORD, PLEASE

Once the site visitor is assured the site is secure, that person often types in a username and a password. The username and password are intended to be used only by a specific individual. That person may then access personal information or perhaps type in credit card information to make a purchase, without unauthorized parties seeing transactions and personal material. Passwords are prizes for cyberthieves, however, so people are advised to change their passwords frequently to make it harder for others to crack into their personal accounts.

Chris Pirillo, the head of LockerGnome, Inc., a network of blogs, web forums, mailing lists, and online communities, has famously said, "Passwords are like

# POWERING UP A CAREER IN INTERNET SECURITY

Cyber thieves are often eager to steal passwords—especially if they unlock credit card and bank account information. Always be careful sharing personal information online, and change your passwords frequently.

underwear: you don't let people see it, you should change it very often, and you shouldn't share it with strangers."

The cybercriminal trying to steal this information might set up a decoy wireless access point and monitor all activity that passes through that connection. Using a scheme such as this, the Internet thief has the potential to steal usernames and passwords, which then may allow him or her to steal funds or make charges on a credit card.

## DEFENDING AGAINST DESTRUCTIVE FORCES, FROM WORMS TO SPIDERS

Another broad category of high-risk threat is malware. Malware includes several different types of software or programs that are intended to hurt or disable computers and computer systems.

A virus, for example, is designed to wreak havoc but not necessarily steal information. When a virus is downloaded into a computer, this malicious program can destroy files, rearrange a hard disk, or cause other damage. It makes sense that these harmful programs are called viruses because they spread like a disease through human interaction. Computer users may unintentionally share an infected file or send an e-mail with a virus attached.

An employee at a major corporation may even be duped into downloading such a malicious program by picking up a USB drive that was purposely dropped in the company parking lot. The curious worker then inserts it into a computer to see the information on it and unleashes a virus that infects his system.

Worms and Trojan horses are also malicious programs designed to damage a computer, but they differ from viruses. A worm can spread without the help of human interaction. It can travel on its own across networks. Some worms have the ability to replicate themselves endlessly and send themselves out to every e-mail address stored in a computer's address book. Some worms allow people to hack into a computer and get full access to data.

A Trojan horse is a program that comes disguised as a tool that may be helpful but its true intent is to corrupt a computer. These programs can also open a doorway to guarded information.

Spyware is also intended to give malevolent parties access to a computer. This is a program that is installed directly in a computer, unbeknownst to the owner.

There are also insidious programs called spiders that crawl through the web looking for valuable data such as e-mails. Spammers may use spiders to capture e-mails and send out either unwanted advertising or scam proposals. These web crawlers and other types of "robots" can be detected in web logs that indicate who has been indexing a site.

These automated programs are also called web bots. Sometimes these bots can take over a group of computers, which is referred to as a "botnet." CAPTCHA is a popular program to protect websites against bots. It typically produces a series of distorted letters that the user then has to retype in to verify that a human is indeed using the system.

## CYBERCRIME HITS THE BIG TIME

Internet security goes beyond those who illegally access personal computers or trick individuals into sharing personal data. On a much larger level, hackers have attacked major companies and corporations.

# SAFETY FIRST IN THE INTERNET AGE

In 2013, hackers cracked into the computer systems of Target stores and made off with the credit and debit card information of up to forty million customers. Potentially, thieves could make fraudulent charges on these cards. In another major heist of customer data, cybercriminals tapped into the computer networks of Home Depot, making off with the personal information from

Shoppers beware! Internet vandals know that major retailers have loads of credit card information. Hackers have stolen customer information from Target, Home Depot, and other major stores.

# POWERING UP A CAREER IN INTERNET SECURITY

fifty-six million shoppers. Similarly, Chase Bank was attacked, affecting seventy-six million households and seven million small businesses.

Other big-name businesses that have been targeted by Internet crooks include Neiman Marcus, Michaels, Dairy Queen, UPS, eBay, and AT&T. Even the U.S. government cannot protect itself from the power of clever hackers.

The White House, the State Department, and the U.S. Postal Service have all been victims of cyberintruders. In the fall of 2014, Russian hackers used a bug in Microsoft Windows to spy on several Western governments, NATO, and the Ukrainian government. For governments, the fears are greater than having financial data stolen. In the wrong hands, sensitive or classified information has the possibility of compromising national security.

As these security breaches have become more common, the need for Internet security experts has become greater than ever.

## NEW TECHNOLOGIES HAVE BROUGHT NEW TARGETS

New cybervulnerabilities have developed as new technologies have come along. More companies and individuals are storing data in the "cloud." Instead of keeping information on computers, the cloud is an option of keeping information on remote servers accessed through the Internet. In 2014, hackers reportedly cracked into Apple's iCloud, accessing users' online storage. The subsequent posting of private celebrity photos was attributed to this cyber break-in.

The Security Assertion Markup Language and related interfaces are the new standard for protecting cloud-based applications.

Mobile devices have also created new security challenges. As more people are connecting to the Internet through their mobile phones, tablets, and other devices, more possible channels have opened up to steal information.

Mobile devices connecting to the Internet through public WiFi networks or hotspots are susceptible to attack. Sometimes some mobile apps will connect to a WiFi network without the user realizing it. Mobile security programs are now designed to provide mobile antivirus and search protection. Some software gives the ability to remotely lock and wipe all data if a device is stolen.

## SOME SAFEGUARDS KEEP TROUBLE AWAY

Despite all the news of security breaches, many safeguards are in place that have been preventing crimes. Firewalls may be one of the most common methods for blocking illegal access to computers. "Firewall" was originally the name for a physical wall that stopped the spread of a fire. Today, it is still a barrier or a shield that can stop people from getting "burned." Firewalls are hardware or software that keeps unrequested Internet traffic from reaching a computer.

The firewall blocks unauthorized entry to a computer or system, but outgoing communication is allowed.

Firewalls are built into most routers today. Many people use routers in their homes to broadcast a WiFi signal that will allow them to access the Internet. The Internet connection typically comes into the home through a modem. The modem is connected to the router. Some modems and computers also have firewalls. Firewalls are usually built into Windows or Mac OS X.

E-mails are somewhat protected by user passwords. Those wanting to protect e-mails may also use encryption programs. Cryptography is a concept that goes back to the days of early Rome. The idea is to disguise a message or information that cannot be understood unless a person has the specific code to decipher the disguised language.

Today, varying methods of cryptography may help protect e-mails. Two organizations that are communicating with each other may use encryption to relay information and keep the data from prying eyes. This type of e-mail encryption, however, is not all that common in everyday use.

Digital signatures and digital certificates can also be used to authenticate messages and identities.

Encryption may be used when accessing financial data. Secure Sockets Layer (SSL) is the standard security technology used for establishing an encrypted link between a web server and a browser. In a secure web session, the web browser generates a random encryption key and sends it to the website host to be matched with its public encryption key. Your browser and the website then encrypt and decrypt all transmissions.

To fight viruses, computer experts have come up with antivirus software that can tell if a computer has been infected. Legitimate virus scanners can detect if there is malware on a system so a user can get rid of it before it destroys files.

## THE SAFETY KEEPERS

Many companies want to hire computer experts who can keep the virtual doors locked. They need trained professionals who know how to keep cyberchannels open to the right individuals but closed tight to those who are not authorized to access them.

In some cases, the hackers who have illegally cracked the systems reform their ways and become the security protectors. Hackers have tremendous skills for navigating computer systems and diagnosing security flaws. Sometimes companies will hire hackers to try and break into their systems to find the weaknesses. Those who put their skills to good use are sometimes called "white hat" hackers, while the "black hat" hackers are criminals, breaking into systems to cause damage or reap financial gain.

The Internet security specialist builds firewalls and installs antivirus software on servers and computers. He or she may keep tabs on all activity going on in a business's computer network, looking vigilantly for any irregularities. Companies that handle sensitive information are major employers of security professionals. These include investment companies, insurance firms, and government agencies.

There is a range of jobs in this field. The cyberdetective investigates a breach in security, trying to track down who perpetrated the crime and how the

# 22 | POWERING UP A CAREER IN INTERNET SECURITY

The people pictured here represent the international activist hacker group known as Anonymous. They are neither black hat nor white hat but target groups, businesses, and government as a means of social protest, or "hacktivism."

cyber break-in was conducted. The Internet security architect designs and builds the protective walls for corporations. Testers make sure the systems are able to thwart malevolent forces. Computer programmers, security engineers, and network analysts are all trained professionals who work in this field. They often work as educators, teaching staff and others on what to be wary of, how to detect the dangers, and how to maintain protection.

## CHAPTER TWO

# SHARPENING THE MIND FOR A SECURITY CAREER

The world of Internet security and hacking combines many skills. Pros in this field enjoy puzzle solving, logic, and creativity. They are the Sherlock Holmeses of the Internet world—able to spot a cybercrime and track down sources of trouble.

Those who succeed in this career typically have an avid interest in math and a firm grasp of many math concepts. Those who truly want to master cybersecurity technology are advised to take advanced mathematics, such as calculus, statistics, and discrete mathematics.

Discrete math is not part of many common high school curriculums, but it especially comes into play in computer work. This branch of math is known as the math of computing, and it has very "real world" applications. Computers rely on discrete math concepts to build fundamental algorithms (sets of rules) that are the foundation of computer programs. Combinatorics, or combinatorial mathematics, falls within the category of discrete mathematics. This subfield involves the selection and arrangement of information. It may be used to figure out the number of possible configurations of discrete items, which is key in programming.

Also, classes that stress communications and writing will prove helpful in this field. Security experts need to clearly explain problems and solutions, which often have to be written out. Any classes related to business may pay off as well. Many security flaws threaten the finances of organizations, so it's important to know how the financial aspects of a company may be structured.

## LEARNING THE LANGUAGE OF COMPUTING

Most students today know how to use a computer, but those who want to explore what it takes to enter the field of Internet security need to dig deeper and find out what makes computers tick. They need to know how computers really work. As they gain an understanding of how these devices and the software they use function, students may modify, adjust, and personalize their computers—because they have the tools and vision to do so.

To get inside the nuts and bolts of how computers operate, some high schools offer courses in computer programming and writing code. Programs and codes are the instructions that tell computers what to do. Programming is key to creating and setting up the protective walls in computing systems.

Computers understand different programming languages. These are methods for giving instructions to a computer. Some of the top computer languages are C, C++, C#, Objective C, Java, Javascript, PHP, SQL, Python, and Ruby.

# SHARPENING THE MIND FOR A SECURITY CAREER | 25

Many students can take computer science courses in their high schools. These classes provide a good foundation for a career in Internet security.

If your high school does not offer programming or coding classes, you can look into private colleges, universities, or community colleges, which may offer computer classes that will earn students credit while they are still in high school. You may want to see what offerings local institutions of higher education may offer. The computer science department at the University of New Mexico has recognized the great need for security

## 26 | POWERING UP A CAREER IN INTERNET SECURITY

experts and holds special training boot camps for high school students to help train them in some basics early on.

## TAPPING INTO SELF-TEACHING SOURCES

If computer training isn't available through any official school programs, check to see if there is an

Most computer jobs require at least some knowledge of computer programming and coding. Students can teach themselves coding through online sources, such as the Hour of Code program.

# SHARPENING THE MIND FOR A SECURITY CAREER | 27

extracurricular computer club in the school or start one. Also, investigate if there is a makerspace in the community. These are spaces where people come together to collaborate on projects that are often tech-oriented. Public libraries may host maker programs or even offer their own free programming lessons.

Students may come together to work on a project that will teach them coding. Arduino, for example, is both a simple coding language and a platform that uses a microcomputer to operate small robotics and other gadgets. Kits are available to build programmable unmanned aerial vehicles and other electronic gizmos.

Many online sources also introduce newcomers to coding and programming. Students might begin to learn about the subject by looking into the Hour of Code program at hourofcode.com. The Hour of Code is a one-hour introduction to computer science, designed to demystify code and show that anybody can learn the basics, and it's available to students around the globe. Code.org also offers many free online lessons. One lesson shows how to get started with Javascript programming. Other exercises demonstrate how to create computer games using code. Another free online resource is Code Academy.

The Institute for Security and Open Methodologies (ISECOM) is a nonprofit technology research company that started an educational program called Hacker High School. This organization has developed lessons for young people to defend themselves against identity theft, malware, and other online attacks. Through exploration and innovation, students learn skills that could help them land a job in the future. Young people

## INTERNSHIPS: GETTING A REAL-WORLD VIEW

To understand what an Internet security job is really like, it's best to be in a real work environment. Those earning a college degree in computing can typically take advantage of their school's internship program. Internships are designed to give students real-world work experience and earn credit. Assisting a cybersecurity team offers the chance to see company-specific security issues up close. Students may research problems and help develop and implement solutions. Working with security pros, you can master the technological terms and grasp the most current problems that are challenging computer protection. Interning also often leads to invaluable job contacts. It's a chance to build your résumé by taking on different responsibilities, and professional connections made at internship may turn into sources for recommendations. In addition, many students find that an internship can be a direct pipeline to full-time employment if they prove themselves to be hard workers, creative thinkers, and team players.

taking lessons through Hacker High School might try to decipher the type of cryptography used in their own messaging programs. They might also determine how Code Red, Nimda, and other famous worms took advantage of software vulnerabilities.

# DIGGING DEEPER INTO CYBERSECURITY

Those who want to build the knowledge needed to be a security pro need to have a handle on basic commands used with popular computer operating systems—Linux, Windows, and OSX. For instance, one command activates the System File Checker in Windows to check if any files are missing or corrupt. Another command will launch the File Signature Verification tool, which can identify which system files are signed and which aren't.

Young hackers are advised to learn the basics of ports and protocols. Ports are access channels through which computers send and receive information. A protocol is a standardized way that data is organized to be transferred. Software in a computer organizes data in a formation called a packet before it is sent.

One of the first lines of defense for any computer system is identification and authentication. Identification may be a username, and authentication may be a password.

Many other websites provide free training specifically in Internet security, including coursera.org and openculture.com. Many sites offer a certificate verifying that a person has completed a series of courses in Internet security.

## MAKING THE COLLEGE CONNECTION

Internet security experts are in high demand, but only the most highly trained land the top jobs. A bachelor's degree in computer science, management information systems, or similar area of study is often the minimum requirement. Because there is such a need for this expertise, colleges have honed their degree programs to equip graduates with skills specific to this field.

College courses specific to cybersecurity may include security technologies and enforcement, statistical analysis of cyberattacks, web technologies, cryptography, and legal issues. There may also be classes that cover steganography, or methods of concealing messages or information within other non-secret text or data.

A few colleges even offer master's degrees in this area for those who may want to specialize in areas such as national security, for example. A curriculum may be designed to instruct about information warfare—the concept that information management and communication technology can be used to gain an advantage over enemies. Those who go into depth on the topic will learn about the psychology of criminal behaviors to become better able to track down the perpetrators of cybercrimes.

While four-year degrees are often preferred by employers, two-year associate's degrees are available in network security, and they can help open the doors to more entry-level positions.

In the IT security field, personal certifications are a great investment. Comptia's Security+ certification, for

## SHARPENING THE MIND FOR A SECURITY CAREER

example, is an industry-recognized certification that has become one of a handful of certifications that are employer-required prerequisites for getting a job at some companies and government agencies. An entry-level certification will help beef up a résumé and serve as a stepping-stone to more advanced certifications. These entry-level certification tests may cost a few

One route to learning Internet security skills is through the U.S. armed forces. The military needs experts to protect the nation's computer networks, and it provides training in return for service.

hundred dollars to take. They are given at test locations throughout the world. International Information Systems Security Certification Consortium also offers professional certification.

One other option to consider that combines both cybersecurity work experience and education is the military. The branches of the U.S. armed forces provide a chance to learn the intricacies of this career through real-life applications and classroom training. Not only does the military pay for training, servicemen and servicewomen earn wages as well.

When it comes to education in cybersecurity, keep this in mind: the learning never stops. As technology keeps evolving, so do security threats. Professionals have to keep up with all the latest advances in technology to succeed.

## CHAPTER THREE

# STARTING OFF IN A SECURITY CAREER

Like many people in technology careers, David Peach got interested in computers when he was young—around the age of eight. He joined his school computer club and experimented at home with computers. Eventually, he earned a college degree in computer science, and after working a few different jobs in the computer field, he wound up as the information security manager for the Economist Group. The company, which includes the *Economist* magazine, focuses on international business and world affairs.

The Economist Group, like so many organizations, relies on security experts like Peach to protect it from attacks on its website and schemes that may be directed at staff or subscribers to falsely get personal or business information.

Some of the criminal activities directed at the company may not be about financial gain but sabotaging editorial content. "Some attackers just want to cause problems for you and your organization by screwing around with your information or systems," Peach says.

To protect subscribers who submit credit card numbers or bank account information, the company outsources the credit card processing to a specialist. The specialist maintains comprehensive

## FROM HACKER TO SECURITY PRO

Criminal hackers are incredibly hard to catch, says David Peach, the information security manager for the Economist Group. "It's not like in real world warfare where you can figure out who is fighting and see where the attack is coming from," he says. "In cyber attacks, it's easy to make it look like the attack is coming from one place, but actually it's coming from somewhere else. Hackers can use a whole chain of computers to obscure where the attack is coming from. That makes it really hard for people like me to find out who is actually doing something."

That said, hackers DO get caught and brought to justice. Some who at first break into computer systems illegally may become legitimate security advisers. Kevin Mitnick, for example, was once called "the most wanted computer criminal in U.S. history." He served a total of six years in prison for hacking into corporate computer systems and stealing secrets. He also breached the national defense warning system. After doing his time, Mitnick became an official security consultant. He says, "The true computer hackers follow a certain set of ethics that forbids them to profit or cause harm from their activities."

## STARTING OFF IN A SECURITY CAREER | 35

Kevin Mitnick was a notorious cyber criminal. He spent six years in prison for stealing computer secrets and breaking into the national defense system. Today, he is an Internet security consultant.

standards established by the Payment Card Industry Security Standards Council to ensure payment card data security.

Peach says that his security analysts spend a good deal of time looking for the types of failures or vulnerabilities that might be exploited by an attacker. "For example, they run tests against the website using the same kinds of tools that the attackers themselves use to look for common vulnerabilities that typically exist," he says.

In addition to searching for flaws, they also continually monitor the website and systems for irregular activity.

"We have a bunch of sensors set up on our network to look out for suspicious things," says Peach.

The security experts are also concerned with attacks on staff. A lot of editorial team members need access to write on the company websites. They create stories on the company blogs and news sites. Peach and his team take steps to ensure passwords are not stolen and viruses are not downloaded. Peach says that an important part of the job is also teaching staff how to be safe.

## GETTING A FOOT IN THE DOOR

Peach works with colleagues who have different levels of experience when it comes to Internet security. While some enter the career fully trained to specifically deal with the most sophisticated security issues, others start in positions where they can learn more about security issues on the job. At some organizations, the role of Internet security is part of another job, such as web master or systems administrator. Some workers may be in jobs that touch upon the subject of security, and then they pursue more training and education, working their way up to being full-fledged security professionals. The important thing starting out is to get any work related to computers and learn as much as possible about networks and systems.

For the most up-to-date information on the average salaries for each type of position, see the Bureau of Labor Statistics website (www.bls.gov) and its *Occupational Outlook Handbook*, or check out the sites of Payscale.com or the InfoSec Institute (http://www.infosecinstitute.com).

# HELP DESK/SUPPORT SPECIALIST

With minimal experience, a person may start off in the security field by working the help desk for an IT (information technology) department at a company. The help desk personnel are on the front lines when it comes to problems, so they often may have the first clue when there is a security issue. Help desk technicians provide assistance to customers or employees who are having a problem with Internet access. Users may call in to report an irregularity, and the help desk technician must be alert to recognize the possibility of security trouble. These professionals are usually well-versed in the software and hardware that support a business. The help desk is a good position to get a sense of the work environment. Help desk technicians may be trained by security management professionals and have an overview of the responsibilities that senior employees take on in building, maintaining, and monitoring security structures.

**Education:** A help desk position may not require specific college training or work experience,

# POWERING UP A CAREER IN INTERNET SECURITY

*A possible starting point for a career in Internet security is at the help or support desk for an IT or information security department.*

although some education in computer programming and computer science can help. An associate's or bachelor's degree in computer science can be a door opener. The job requires strong people skills and problem-solving abilities. From this position, a help desk technician may advance to a position as an IT security specialist.

# WEB DEVELOPER/DESIGNER

Professionals who construct websites must have some knowledge of Internet security. The web is the entry point for cybercriminals, so web developers need to comprehend systems that can be set up to keep users safe and thwart the efforts of those seeking ill gain. Certain features on a website make it more susceptible to attacks—chat areas, electronic commerce, and automatic e-mail responses. The more users can interact with a website, the more vulnerable to attack it may be.

Web design brings together many skills, including computer programming and graphic design. The site creators know how to incorporate animation, video, audio, and interactive features. As these professionals construct a site, they have to keep in mind the elements that may be susceptible to hackers and make sure safety measures are in place. If there is a page where users have to put in personal and financial information, a web page should have elements in place that adhere to the payment card industry (American Express, Discover Financial Services, JCB International, MasterCard Worldwide, and Visa Inc.) standards. All entities that store, process, or transmit cardholder data have to abide by these standards. Some of these safeguards include proper firewall configuration to protect cardholder data, encryption of transmitted cardholder data, restrictions on access to sensitive information, the use of unique IDs to access material,

# POWERING UP A CAREER IN INTERNET SECURITY

Web developers know the nuts and bolts of how websites are built and operate. These professionals sometimes gather at conferences to share ideas and make career connections.

the means to track and monitor all access to a network, and methods to regularly test security systems.

**Education:** Beginning web designers can often get entry-level work while working toward a degree. Colleges offer two-year associate's degrees and four-year diplomas in this subject.

# COMPUTER OPERATOR/ TECHNICIAN

The roles of computer operator and technician can often overlap. These workers monitor and operate computers and related data-processing equipment. The extent of their duties varies depending on the organization. They may check that all computers in a network are operating correctly and check the status of wires and connections to the Internet. They help ensure that monitors, keyboards, and printers are all in working order. In general, the computer operators are more in tune with hardware than software, but in reviewing the status of equipment, they may spot signs of a security breach. They may run checks on firewalls and update anti-spam and anti-phishing programs. Operators and technicians may help clean up computer systems and make sure they are running as efficiently as possible. Depending on their level of experience, they may handle electronic repairs and configurations. Sometimes, people seeking work in this field may start to gain experience by working in an electronics retail store, such as Best Buy, advising consumers on how to set up systems in their homes or small businesses.

**Education:** Some may start in a computer operator or technician position with only a high school diploma, but a computer science–related education can help secure a position. Some employers prefer at least a two-year degree.

## CHAPTER FOUR

# TAKING A STEP UP

For those who want to get more involved with cybersecurity, there are positions dealing more extensively with implementing the software and systems that computers need to operate. These jobs often involve security duties or build a solid foundation for getting an advanced position in security.

## NETWORK AND SYSTEMS ADMINISTRATOR

In the career ladder, this position is a step up from technician. These professionals oversee the computer systems in an organization. They may have technicians working for them to help maintain operations and take quick action when there is trouble. They take care of malfunctions in hardware and software; some of these problems may be the result of breaks in Internet security. They may configure all internal systems such as net routers and firewalls. They may be in charge of company servers, including any web servers. Servers are computers dedicated to storing and providing data, and they are accessed by multiple users. Some administrators may also maintain and build the systems for telecommunications networks so employees can log into office systems while they are at home or on the road. This type of communication also poses another type of security threat. In terms of titles, network administrators may also be network engineers. Network engineers are the professionals who actually set up all the systems, and administrators

Servers are the lifeblood of a computer network. They store, receive, and transmit data. IT engineers and network administrators are often in charge of these vital computers.

## TEACH YOURSELF

While college classes may be one of the best ways to gain computer skills, those who are driven to succeed in this field may also consider approaches to self-learning. Several sites and programs online offer lessons on how to learn to code. The ambitious can figure out how to set up a home network of a few computers and follow instructional material on how to secure that network. With a secure network in play, one can attempt to hack into that system. Hands-on experimentation and tinkering can be an excellent approach to learning. Another affordable option to learn about Internet security may be volunteering time to a charity or another organization that is seeking to set up a secure network. Volunteering provides an invaluable public service as well as an opportunity to gain real-world experience that will certainly look good on a résumé.

oversee the systems and decide how they will be set up. Often, those in the field wear both hats—that of administrator and engineer.

**Education:** Employers may prefer to hire those with some higher education or a bachelor's degree in computer science. Certification may be a requirement for some employers. For example, there are classes to become a Cisco Certified Internetwork Expert.

# PROGRAMMER

Programmers are sometimes called code monkeys because they continually type in all the code needed to make software and computer systems operate. They make sure the code makes sense and will function correctly. However, they are not always the ones involved with the concept or design of a program. They typically take the program designs created by software developers and engineers and make them into the instructions that a computer can follow. The job requires clear, concise, and error-free work. In the world of security, programmers may be working on developing encryption programs that will help keep data disguised and only allow it to be deciphered if running the appropriate program. If they have worked on security-related programs, they may have a sense of how they operate and what security flaws there may be. This type of knowledge can help them advance to more senior positions in information security.

**Education:** Programmers often earn a bachelor's degrees in computer programming or computer science, but some employers will hire those with a two-year diploma in this subject. Many of the courses are devoted to programming languages such as C, Javascript, Python, Ruby, and others.

# POWERING UP A CAREER IN INTERNET SECURITY

To hone their computer skills, programmers may participate in events called hackathons, where computer scientists can work together to create programs that will help find computer bugs.

## SOFTWARE DEVELOPER

Sometimes referred to as software engineers, these professionals are the creative brains who actually come up with programs. They often start as programmers and advance to becoming software developers. They envision and build the applications that perform certain tasks or allow people to perform tasks. In the world of Internet security, they may create software that can block or detect computer viruses or provide spyware and firewalls. Some software will offer identity theft prevention, anti-phishing functions, and online backup. The developers are the visionaries, and they rely on teamwork to get things done. They are experts at identifying problems and coming up with solutions. Once they develop the software, they test and evaluate it to make any corrections or improvements.

**Education:** Typically, software developers have a bachelor's degree in computer science and strong computer programming skills. Software developers may be involved in selling and marketing their creations, so education in accounting, business, or finance can help. Communication and people skills are essential.

**CHAPTER FIVE**

# MEET THE A-TEAM: SECURITY SPECIALISTS

While Internet security may be one of the duties of a network administrator or other computer professional, security has become such an important issue for organizations that very specific careers have developed that address these safety concerns. Opportunities are emerging faster than trained workers who can fill these positions. Those at the top of this field are in very high demand and command high salaries to match.

## INFORMATION SECURITY ANALYST/MANAGER

Like David Peach at the Economist Group, these professionals are experts in cybersecurity. They are fully educated on all the types of protection to strengthen networks and computers, and they are continually staying informed about the latest web attacks and how they were executed. These senior-level experts know how to recognize possible breaches in security, possibly locate the source of the trouble, determine how to best correct any damage, and then set up the safeguards that will prevent such an attack from happening again.

## MEET THE A-TEAM: SECURITY SPECIALISTS | 49

Black hat hackers may be the bad guys, but the Black Hat Conference is about defending computers from attacks. Internet specialists attend such events to learn the latest in security threats.

A first step for these specialists is often to assess the materials that are at risk, whether they are financial data, e-mails, or articles and information that can be hacked and distorted. They review what security measures (firewalls, antivirus programs, data encryption, etc.) are already in place. Also, analysts are fully informed on the current standards for protection, such as the payment card industry data security standards. Then they develop a defense plan, including how to continually monitor and test the system for vulnerabilities. If working with a Microsoft system, for example, a network can be monitored with Network Monitor. Also known as NetMon, this utility can be used to capture and observe network traffic patterns and problems. Because cybercriminals keep finding ways to illegally break into systems via the Internet, security analysts are continually learning and updating systems within their organizations. They may even set up a computer system on the Internet called a "honey pot." Its sole purpose is to trap the cyberthieves who attempt to break into other people's computer systems. Managers also continually teach staff how they can best prepare themselves and their computers against attacks.

**Education:** Typically, these analysts will have at least a bachelor's in computer science, programming, or engineering. Some bachelor's degree program focus specifically on network and information systems security. Professional organizations dedicated to computer security also offer certification, which many employers now want as proof that an analyst is fully educated in the latest technology related to web safety.

## INFORMATION SECURITY CRIME INVESTIGATOR/ FORENSICS EXPERT

These specialists are the dedicated detectives of the Internet policing world. This job falls under the broad category of computer forensics. These pros know how to search for and recover digital evidence of crimes. They may be called upon for court cases involving fraud, espionage, and cybervandalism. They may also be able to find evidence for cases involving child pornography and even murder. The forensics experts may be able to uncover search histories and deleted e-mails that indicate heinous intent. They gather the digital evidence that may prove the crimes of a computer intruder. They pinpoint the scene of the crimes—the computers or systems that have been compromised—and detail times, methods, and information stolen or disrupted.

A company may start to receive a series of complaints from customers who report that suspicious e-mails from the company are popping up in their in-boxes asking them to go to a site that resembles the company payment page and put in personal financial information. The forensics expert is put in charge of tracing the source of the scheme and putting together the evidence to build a case against the perpetrators. The work involves very detailed accounting of the who, why, when, where, what, and how of a crime. If a court trial comes about, evidence must be shown to be authentic, reliably obtained, and admissible in court.

**Education:** A bachelor's degree related to computer science is the minimum requirement. Forensic accounting is a related field that may benefit the computer forensic professional. The field involves the analysis and investigation of financial and business data that are part of a criminal case. This is a developing field, but it is vital to have knowledge of the law, the legal system, and the latest rulings related to cybercrimes. Several certifications

## A KIDNAPPING SOLVED THROUGH CYBER DETECTIVE WORK

Sometimes being able to break through or decipher online security issues can solve serious, life-endangering crimes. When Scott Tyree kidnapped a thirteen-year-old girl in 2002, he sent a photo of the kidnapped girl via instant message to someone who knew him only by his Yahoo! screen name. By not using his real identity, the kidnapper thought he could not get caught. The man who received the photo reported Tyree to the FBI. Detectives contacted Yahoo! and found the IP address belonging to the Yahoo! screen name. IP, or Internet protocol, addresses allow one computer (or other digital device) to communicate with another through the Internet. Verizon had the subscriber name and address of the person who had been assigned the IP address. The FBI were then quickly able to rescue the girl and arrest Scott Tyree.

that prove competency are available from organizations such as the International Society of Forensic Computer Examiners, the Information Assurance Certification Review Board, and the International Association of Computer Investigative Specialists. These certifications

## MEET THE A-TEAM: SECURITY SPECIALISTS

John Hair (pictured here) is a cybercrime expert. Sometimes, Internet security specialists need to appear in court to provide evidence and expertise to prosecute cyber thugs.

are often recognized as official credentials in a court of law or with law enforcement personnel. Some software companies provide their own certification classes for their proprietary forensics software. Guidance Software, for example, has the EnCase Certified Examiner (EnCE) credential, and AccessData offers the AccessData Certified Examiner (ACE) certification.

# POWERING UP A CAREER IN INTERNET SECURITY

54

## WEB PENETRATION TESTER

In a sense, these are the "good guys" or legal hackers who know how to use code and programming to test the security of existing computer systems. Sometimes called pen testers, they try to break into systems and get paid good money to do so. They try to think like the "bad guys," and figure out what information they

To be in Internet security, you often have to think like a hacker. Web penetration testers try to break into computer systems to test if their security defenses are working.

## MEET THE A-TEAM: SECURITY SPECIALISTS

might want to tamper with or steal. Then, they go about trying to do just that. They often have to think outside of the box in order to spot weaknesses and flaws. They try to find the holes in Internet barriers, before the criminals do. Based on their results, they can suggest further ways for organizations to beef up their security. Also referred to as cyber penetration testers, they may use tools such as web application vulnerability scanners. They review usage logs and analyze sessions (website usage). They work with the top security team members. When they find flaws, they have to describe the problems and present detailed options for tightening security.

**Education:** A bachelor's degree in computer science is recommended along with a strong knowledge of programming languages, such as Javascript and Python. It's helpful to have a solid base in website design as well. Certifications, such as the Global Information Assurance Certification for Web Application Penetration Tester, are available.

CHAPTER SIX

# SECURING A JOB IN INTERNET SECURITY

To unlock the right opportunity in Internet security, job seekers need a strategy and the right tools to convince employers to hire them.

When it's time to hunt for a job in the cybersafety field, one of the first questions may be "Where do you want to work?" So many businesses and organizations now depend on security authorities that a job seeker may want to decide on the type of operation that most closely matches his or her personal interests. Corporations dealing with sports, film, television, health care, science, technology, finance, architecture, insurance, and more may have sensitive information that needs protecting.

This is also a career with global opportunities, so applicants may have the luxury of finding work anywhere in the world. Although many opportunities may be in big cities, openings in this field are available in many smaller communities as well.

## UNCOVERING OPPORTUNITIES

It doesn't take long to search for and find job opportunities for security experts online. The major online job-listing sites such as Indeed, SimplyHired, Vault, CareerBuilder, and Monster all present

# SECURING A JOB IN INTERNET SECURITY | 57

The Internet is, naturally, a great place for job hunters to start searching for opportunities in Internet security. Many sites offer connections to employers who are seeking talent.

openings in this field. Other sites are specifically geared toward technology jobs, such as Dice, Robert Half Technology, and Harvey Nash.

Many companies that develop security software and systems may be worth looking into. For those interested in building the security products, check into businesses like BitArmor Systems, which produces software that protects stored data, or Cryptolex Trust Systems, which creates authentication methods for mobile devices. FireEye is another major security software company. Checkpoint Software Technologies specializes in firewall software. Guidance Software focuses on products that track down the culprits of hacking or identity theft and helping to repair the damage.

Cisco is one of the giants in business security with products for cloud security, secure router hardware, and integrated security. Symantec is also a major player, best known for its antivirus software Norton, and it may be one of the most-used certificate authorities.

All the corporations that have made headlines for security lapses are in need of security professionals—Sony, Target, Home Depot, etc. Some of the top corporations that have recruited cybersecurity specialists in the past have been Northrop Grumman, General Dynamics, Science Applications International Corporation, ManTech International, PricewaterhouseCoopers, Booz Allen Hamilton, Hewlett-Packard, Dell, and Accenture.

Recruiters are eager to work with security specialists. They often do the legwork and contact job seekers directly.

Also, never underestimate the power of networking. Friends, family, and former work mates may know of opportunities, and their recommendations can make the difference between getting a job and being shown the door. LinkedIn is a site dedicated to helping job seekers find networking connections.

Mentors are great networking sources as well. A mentor is a seasoned professional in your field who is willing to give advice and guidance and share life lessons about the career.

# THE TOOLS TO BREAK INTO THE JOB

As in any job hunt, the résumé must be perfectly constructed. Employers need to be able to quickly understand qualifications, work history, and education.

Résumés can have different structures, but for those in the tech field it's essential to stress tech skills.

Career fairs can be efficient ways to explore employment possibilities. At these events, employers and job seekers connect and share information.

## LESSONS FROM FIRST JOBS AND TEMP POSITIONS

For those just starting in their working life, it's important to make the most of a first job. The first job can provide many of the elements needed to build a résumé. It may be an opportunity to demonstrate teamwork, leadership skills, punctuality, and the ability to work hard. Even if a first job isn't perfect, it can help a person know what he or she doesn't like and focus on priorities. The first job teaches lessons about working with others—fellow employees, customers, and a supervisor. If a permanent job isn't immediately available, consider temp work. Temporary employment allows people to try different work environments. They can possibly learn new work skills and make valuable networking connections. If a temp worker performs well on the job, it can lead to a permanent position.

Highlight experience in programming and mention all programming languages in which you're fluent. Spotlight your familiarity with security technologies, such as antivirus programs (Norton, for example), digital security certificates, and security scanners. Underscore knowledge of systems (Unix, Windows, etc.)

and networks and their related technologies (firewalls, routers, wide area networks or WANs, local area networks or LANs, etc.).

When summarizing work experience, point out achievements. What were security gaps you discovered? How were they corrected? What was at stake? How many identities were protected? How much was potentially prevented from being stolen?

The résumé needs to convey that the job candidate has the abilities that employers are seeking. It may include examples of teamwork, self-starting, and leadership. Education should include any higher education degrees as well as any certifications.

## DON'T NEGLECT COVER LETTERS AND RECOMMENDATIONS

Cover letters are a chance to tell employers about experience and skills that may not be on the résumé. They also allow job applicants an opportunity to directly explain why they are strong candidates for a position. The cover letter should convey curiosity, personality, and interest.

Recommendations may be required. These letters describe the professional relationship the writer had with the job seeker and highlight achievements. The letter may underscore personal strengths and tangible skills. A recommender gives examples of leadership and teamwork. Some human resource workers ask for references and not written recommendations. References

# POWERING UP A CAREER IN INTERNET SECURITY

are also people who have had a professional relationship with the job candidate, and they have to be ready to sing the praises of a job applicant when HR calls.

## THE INTERVIEW HURDLE

If an employer is suitably impressed by the résumé, cover letter, and recommendations, the job candidate

The interview is a last but important hurdle to get over when applying for a job. This meeting gives a job candidate a chance to make an impression in person.

may make it to the next level in the hiring process: the interview. The interview is a chance to sit down face-to-face with those who do the hiring. Employers want to get a sense of the applicant as a real person. It's a chance to show poise, confidence, and personal skills. It's a job candidate's chance to sell himself or herself. (Don't forget to come dressed for success.) Emphasize skills, personal traits, and accomplishments. It's also a chance to ask an employer any questions about the position.

Here is a sample of some possible interview questions that may be asked for any tech position:

- How do you stay current with technical skills and knowledge?
- What has been your greatest challenge, and how did you handle it?
- What security problems have you dealt with?
- What changes have you implemented in previous jobs?
- What is an example of how you applied your technical knowledge?

## CHAPTER SEVEN

# THE FUTURE OF INTERNET SECURITY

The Internet may never be 100 percent secure. New security structures that are introduced seem to be continually knocked down.

In the spring of 2014, researchers discovered a flaw in the widely used encryption technology called SSL (Secure Sockets Layer). SSL has been a standard security technology for establishing an encrypted link between a web server and a browser. It is used with many websites that collect personal and financial information. A small coding error in SSL—dubbed Heartbleed—was detected, and it had the potential to threaten many Internet users. The discovery sent companies scrambling to update their security practices.

## NEW DANGERS, NEW OPPORTUNITIES

Heartbleed is one of several examples of how "safe" cyberwalls continue to be toppled. Although it is bad news for users, it may be good news for Internet security specialists—keeping them in high demand when it comes to employment. As a result of flaws like Heartbleed, credit card companies are continuously looking to set new standards that will ensure customer confidentiality.

## THE FUTURE OF INTERNET SECURITY | 65

The government and the military are especially concerned about hacking and are wary of an unexpected massive attack on their computers that they fear could be a digital Pearl Harbor, destroying or compromising vital information. Or perhaps a big enough attack could shut down Wall Street or falsify stock market information. People are taking as many precautionary measures as possible to prevent such disasters.

Cybersecurity is vital to the nation's security. National Security Agency director Mike Rogers explains to a crowd at Stanford University why the country needs computer security specialists.

Some experts predict that one approach increasing online safety may be through the use of biometrics. Biometrics refers to technologies that use physical traits for identification purposes. Passwords of the future may be scans of the retina, fingerprints, or voice patterns. Whatever security looks like in the years to come, some fear that only the rich will be able to access the best forms of security.

In the summer of 2014, the Pew Research Center published "Net Threats," the third in a series called "Digital Life in 2025." In the survey of 1,400 high-profile technology thinkers, concerns were expressed that the future of the Internet will include greater surveillance and less trust online.

## THE INTERNET OF THINGS

Many envision a world where almost everything in the world will be accessible through computers and possibly the Internet. Cars, bridges, street lights, and garbage bins may all be outfitted with components that let them respond to signals and send information back to a computer or other electronic devices.

The idea could be put to good use. If cars were fitted with sensors or streetlights could monitor traffic, computers may have the potential to provide fast analysis of traffic movement and adjust traffic lights accordingly, citywide, to ease congestion.

As this Internet of Things spreads, cyberexperts who are trying to stay one step ahead of criminal activity have envisioned more elaborate techno-crimes. At the DefCon computer security conferences in Las Vegas in

## THE FUTURE OF INTERNET SECURITY

### HACK A HEART ATTACK?

One frightening hacking possibility in the future sounds like it comes out of a science fiction novel. Some cyber pros have warned that pacemakers and other implantable devices may be hacked so as to actually kill a person. Programming genius Barnaby Jack believed in this idea. Jack had already demonstrated how to hack into an ATM to dispense cash. He was due to make a presentation on how pacemakers could be controlled via computer technology when he died at age thirty-five.

2013, cybersecurity professionals demonstrated how hybrid cars that employ computer technology could be taken over and controlled from afar by hackers. The cars could be digitally hijacked from the driver—steered, sped up, slowed down, or stopped through new technology. Security pros at the conference warned that more new cars may be equipped with Internet connections, and this would make attacks easier. In February 2015, a fourteen-year-old boy demonstrated how he could remotely unlock and start a car using $15 worth of equipment that he had purchased at an electronics store. Auto representatives were stunned.

New home security systems that can be operated via wireless connections are not impervious. The tech savvy

# POWERING UP A CAREER IN INTERNET SECURITY

*Internet security is a field rich in opportunity. As long as hackers continue to break through cyber safeguards, cybersecurity professionals will be needed to protect the world's information.*

can infiltrate these systems and make doors open without a crowbar but with few button pushes.

With all these new worlds of interconnectivity on the horizon, Internet security careers are here to stay because the security of any system cannot yet be guaranteed.

Professor Gene Spafford, a computer security expert form Purdue University, says in an article titled "Computer Recreations: Of Worms, Viruses and Core War," that "the only truly secure system is one that is powered off, cast in a block of concrete and sealed in a lead-lined room with armed guards."

# GLOSSARY

**browser** Software application or interface used to view websites. Some top browsers are Mozilla Firefox, Internet Explorer, and Google Chrome.

**certificate authority** A trusted entity that issues digital certificates that are proof that an identity is authentic. An SSL certificate, for example, ensures that there can be a secure session between a browser and a web server.

**digital signature** A digital code that is attached to an e-mail or electronic document and provides proof of the sender's identity.

**encryption** The act of encoding data that one computer is sending to another, putting it into a form that only the other computer will be able to decipher.

**firewall** Hardware or software in a computer system that is designed to prevent unauthorized access. The firewall allows or blocks traffic into and out of a system.

**hacker** An expert of computer systems and programming languages who typically knows how to gain unauthorized access to computer systems. White hat hackers use their talents for good—testing computer systems, identifying weaknesses, and suggesting security solutions. Black hat hackers break into computer systems illegally to steal or sabotage information.

**HTML** Hypertext markup language. The computer coding language used to create web pages. HTML provides instructions about a web page's format and what is to be displayed on the page.

**HTTP** Hypertext transfer protocol. A set of rules that controls and allows web browsers and servers to communicate and exchange information. URLs of websites typically begin with http://. A secure connection will present itself as https://.

**IP address** Every device that accesses the web has an IP address assigned to it. This is a distinct line of numbers separated by periods that identifies the apparatus. For example, the numbers may be 66.212.64.164.

**malware** Short for malicious software, these programs gain illegal access to a computer with the intent of disrupting a system or illegally gathering private information. Viruses, worms, Trojan horses, and spyware are all different types of malware.

**phishing** Sending e-mails that fraudulently claim to represent a legitimate organization and then lure the user to a scam website that requests personal information that may be used for financial gain or identify theft.

**server** In the Internet world, a server is a dedicated computer that stores web page information and then serves (or delivers) it to the user.

**spam** Unsolicited junk e-mail sent out in mass mailings.

**SSL** Secure Sockets Layer. Standard technology for establishing a safe, encrypted link between a browser and a server. It is designed to keep all data passed between browser and server confidential. SSL is often used on pages designed for financial transactions that may ask for credit card or bank account information.

# GLOSSARY | 71

**Trojan horse** A malicious virus that is disguised as a seemingly harmless program. When downloaded onto a computer, it can cause serious damage to a computer system.

**URI and URL** Universal resource identifier and universal resource locator. URLs are a subset of URIs. A URI identifies a resource by location, name, or both, but the more specific URLs are the specific web addresses most of us use today to access the network location of a specific resource.

**virus** A malicious program or piece of code that a computer user downloads without his or her knowledge and/or because of deceptive means. When the virus infects a computer, it can change or remove application and system files and possibly make the computer inoperable. Antivirus software is designed to identify and stop viruses.

**web bot** An automated program that lets an attacker take over a computer. The computer then responds to the commands of the attacker. The victim devices are often called "zombies." These bots spread throughout the Internet looking for unprotected computers to attack. Some bots are called web crawlers or spiders.

**worm** A type of malware that replicates itself and spreads to other computers.

# FOR MORE INFORMATION

Canadian Advanced Technology Alliance (CATA)
207 Bank Street, Suite 416
Ottawa, ON K2P 2N2
Canada
(613) 236-6550
Website: http://www.cata.ca
The largest high-tech association in Canada, CATA is a comprehensive resource with the latest high-tech news in Canada.

MediaSmarts
950 Gladstone Avenue, Suite 120
Ottawa, ON K1Y 3E6
Canada
(613) 224-7721
Website: http://mediasmarts.ca
A Canadian not-for-profit organization for digital and media literacy, with helpful resources on these subjects, MediaSmarts's work falls into the areas of education, public awareness, and research and policy.

National Association of Programmers
P.O. Box 529
Prairieville, LA 70769
Website: http://www.napusa.org
This group is dedicated to providing information and resources to help programmers, developers, consultants, and students in the computer industry.

# FOR MORE INFORMATION | 73

OpenMedia
1424 Commercial Drive
P.O. Box 21674
Vancouver, BC V5L 5G3
Canada
(604) 633-2744
Website: http://openmedia.ca
OpenMedia is a Canadian grassroots organization that safeguards the possibilities of an open and affordable Internet.

TryComputing.org
445 Hoes Lane
Piscataway, NJ 08854-4141
(732) 981-0060
Website: http://www.trycomputing.org/inspire/computing-student-opportunities
This site from the Institute of Electrical and Electronics Engineers features competitions, events, internships, and research programs for young people. Also find out about career opportunities and colleges with computer programming courses.

## WEBSITES

Because of the changing nature of Internet links, Rosen Publishing has developed an online list of websites related to the subject of this book. This site is updated regularly. Please use this link to access the list:

http://www.rosenlinks.com/PTC/Inter

# FOR FURTHER READING

Campagna, Rich, Subbu Iyer, and Ashwin Krishnan. *Mobile Device Security for Dummies.* Hoboken, NJ: Wiley Publishing, 2011.

Cline, Ernest. *Ready Player One.* New York, NY: Broadway Books, 2012.

Crowder, David. *Building a Web Site for Dummies.* Hoboken, NJ: Wiley Publishing, 2010.

Doctorow, Cory. *Little Brother.* New York, NY: Macmillan, 2008.

Farrell, Mary. *Computer Programming for Teens.* Boston, MA: Thomas Course Technology, 2008.

Ford, Jerry Lee. *Programming for the Absolute Beginner.* Boston, MA: Thomson Course Technology, 2007.

Freedman, Jeri. *Careers in Computer Science and Programming.* New York, NY: Rosen Classroom, 2011.

Frieder, Ophir. *Computer Science Programming Basics in Ruby.* Sebastapol, CA: O'Reilly Media: 2013.

Grant, Michael. *BZRK.* New York, NY: Egmont, 2012.

Ivester, Mark. *lol...OMG!: What Every Student Needs to Know About Online Reputation Management, Digital Citizenship and Cyberbullying.* Reno, NV: Serra Knight Publishing, 2011.

Kim, Peter. *The Hacker Playbook: Practical Guide to Penetration Testing.* North Charleston, SC: Secure Planet, 2014.

Levy, Steven. *Hackers: Heroes of the Computer Revolution—25th Anniversary Edition.* Sebastopol, CA: O'Reilly Media, 2010.

# FOR FURTHER READING

Lloyd, Ian. *Build Your Own Web Site the Right Way Using HTML & CSS.* 2nd ed. Collingwood, Australia: Site Point Pty, 2008.

Marques, Marcelo. *Hackerteen: Volume 1: Internet Blackout.* Sebastopol, CA: O'Reilly Media, 2009.

McCarthy, Linda. *Own Your Space: Keep Yourself and Your Stuff Safe Online.* Redmond, WA: Microsoft, 2011.

Mitnick, Kevin. *Ghost in the Wires: My Adventures as the World's Most Wanted Hacker.* New York, NY: Back Bay Books, 2012.

Poulsen, Kevin. *Kingpin: How One Hacker Took Over the Billion-Dollar Cybercrime Underground.* New York, NY: Broadway Books, 2012.

Robbins, Jennifer Nierderst. *Learning Web Design: A Beginner's Guide to HTML, CSS, JavaScript, and Web Graphics.* Sebastapol, CA: O'Reilly Media: 2012.

Sande, Warren, and Carter Sande. *Hello World! Computer Programming for Kids and Other Beginners.* Greenwich, CT: Manning, 2009.

Sandler, Corey. *Living with the Internet and Online Dangers.* New York, NY: Facts On File, 2010.

Sethi, Maneesh. *Game Programming for Teens.* Boston, MA: Thomson Course Technology, 2009.

Zalewski, Michal. *The Tangled Web: A Guide to Securing Modern Web Applications.* San Francisco, CA: No Starch Press, 2011.

# BIBLIOGRAPHY

Bilodeau, Anne. "Hacking the Web: A Security Guide." Webdeveloper.com. Retrieved January 18, 2015 (http://www.webdeveloper.com/security/security_hacking_the_web.html).

Bilton, Nick. "Disruptions: As New Targets for Hackers, Your Car and Your House." *New York Times*, August 11, 2013. Retrieved January 18, 2015 (http://bits.blogs.nytimes.com/2013/08/11/taking-over-cars-and-homes-remotely/?_r=1).

Delker, Kim. "Hacking for a Good Cause." The University of New Mexico, July 25, 2014. Retrieved January 18, 2015 (http://news.unm.edu/news/hacking-for-a-good-cause).

Doyle, Allison. "Interview Questions for Tech Jobs." About Careers. Retrieved January 18, 2015 (http://jobsearch.about.com/od/tech/a/tech-interview-questions.htm).

Dunn, Nash. "A New Breed of Security." The ONE, October 14, 2011. Retrieved January 18, 2015 (http://www.observernewsonline.com/content/new-breed-security).

Hacker High School. "Cyber Security Skills for the Real World." Retrieved January 18, 2015 (http://www.hackerhighschool.org).

How-to Geek. "5 Serious Problems with HTTPS and SSL Security on the Web." Retrieved January 18, 2015 (http://www.howtogeek.com/182425/5-serious-problems-with-https-and-ssl-security-on-the-web).

IT Security Column. "Top 10 IT Security Quotes."

# BIBLIOGRAPHY | 77

Retrieved January 18, 2015 (http://www.itscolumn.com/2011/08/top-10-it-security-quotes).

National Center for Education Statistics. "Protecting Your System: Network (Internet) Security." Retrieved January 18, 2015 (http://nces.ed.gov/pubs98/safetech/chapter9.asp).

*Occupational Outlook Handbook.* "Information Security Analysts." Retrieved January 18, 2015 (http://www.bls.gov/ooh/computer-and-information-technology/information-security-analysts.htm).

Patrick, David. "Why Discrete Math Is Important." Art of Problem Solving. Retrieved January 18, 2015 (http://www.artofproblemsolving.com/Resources/articles.php?page=discretemath).

Peach, David. Interview with author. January 8, 2015.

Ravenscraft, Eric. "What We Can Learn from the Biggest Corporate Hacks." Lifehacker, December 16, 2014. Retrieved January 18, 2015 (http://lifehacker.com/what-we-can-learn-from-the-biggest-corporate-hacks-1671682353).

Symantec-Norton. "The 11 Most Common Computer Security Threats… And What You Can Do to Protect Yourself from Them." Retrieved January 18, 2015 (http://www.symantec-norton.com/11-most-common-computer-security-threats_k13.aspx).

Winkler, Ira. "How to Get a Job in Cyber Security." Computerworld, September 8, 2014. Retrieved January 18, 2015 (http://www.computerworld.com/article/2603927/security0/how-to-get-a-job-in-computer-security.html).

# INDEX

## B

Berners-Lee, Tim, 9–10
businesses, cyberattacks on, 16–18, 58

## C

cloud, the, 18–19, 58
computer operator/technician, 41

## E

education, 23–32, 37–38, 40, 41, 44–45, 47, 50, 51–53, 55
encryption, 6, 12, 20, 39, 45, 49, 64

## F

firewalls, 6, 19–20, 21, 22, 39, 41, 42, 47, 49, 58
forensics experts, 50–53

## H

hackers, 6, 16–18, 21, 34, 39, 54, 58, 65
help desk/support specialist, 37–38

## I

identity theft, 27, 47, 58
imposter sites, 12–13, 51
information security analyst/manager, 48–50
information security crime investigator, 50–53
Internet, how it works, 8–10
Internet security
  careers in, 21–22, 37–41, 42–47, 48–55
  future of, 64–68
  getting a job in, 56–63
  importance of, 4–7, 21–22, 33–36
  preparing for a career in, 23–32
  secure websites, 11–12
internships, 28
interviews, job, 62–63

## M

malware, 15–16

## N

network analysts, 22
network and system administrators, 42–45
network engineers, 43–44

## P

passwords, 13–15, 29, 36, 66
Peach, David, 33–36, 48
phishing, 12, 41, 47
programmers, 22, 45

## R

résumés, 59–61

## S

security architects, 22
security engineers, 22
security specialists, 48–55
software developers, 45, 46–47

## T

spiders, 16
spyware, 16, 47

Trojan horses, 15, 16

## V

viruses, 15, 20–21, 36, 47, 49, 58

## W

web developer/designer, 39–40
web penetration testers, 22, 54–55
worms, 15–16

## ABOUT THE AUTHOR

Don Rauf is the author of several books about technology, including *Getting the Most Out of Makerspaces to Explore Arduino*, *Getting the Most Out of Makerspaces to Build Unmanned Aerial Vehicles*, and *Getting to Know Hackety Hack*. He has also written books on career success and numerous other topics.

## PHOTO CREDITS

Cover bikeriderlondon/Shutterstock.com; cover (background), back cover, p. 1 spaxiax/Shutterstock.com; p. 5 Leigh Vogel/WireImage/Getty Images; p. 11 KTSDesign/Science Photo Library/Getty Images; p. 14 davidgoldmanphoto/Image Source/Getty Images; pp. 17, 59 Bloomberg/Getty Images; pp. 22, 31, 40, 49, 54, 65 © AP Images; p. 25 © Pat Vasquez-Cunningham/Albuquerque Journal/ZUMA Press; p. 26 John Leyba/The Denver Post/Getty Images; p. 35 Craig F. Walker/The Denver Post/Getty Images; p. 38 Ronnie Kaufman/Larry Hirschowitz/Blend Images/Getty Images; p. 43 Baran Özdemir/Vetta/Getty Images; p. 46 The Washington Post/Getty Images; p. 53 Pool/Getty Images; p. 57 Zak Kendal/Cultura/Getty Images; p. 62 Nick White and Fiona Jackson-Downes/Cultura/Getty Images; p. 68 Paolo Cipriani/E+/Getty Images; cover and interior pages design elements Zffoto/Shutterstock.com, Sergey Nivens/Shutterstock.com, elen_studio/Shutterstock.com, Lukas Rs/Shutterstock.com, Nucleartist/Shutterstock.com, Georg Preissl/Shutterstock.com, Jack1e/Shutterstock.com, Sfio Cracho/Shutterstock.com.

Designer: Michael Moy; Editor: Shalini Saxena

Porter County Public Library